*I pray for a life of going nowhere*

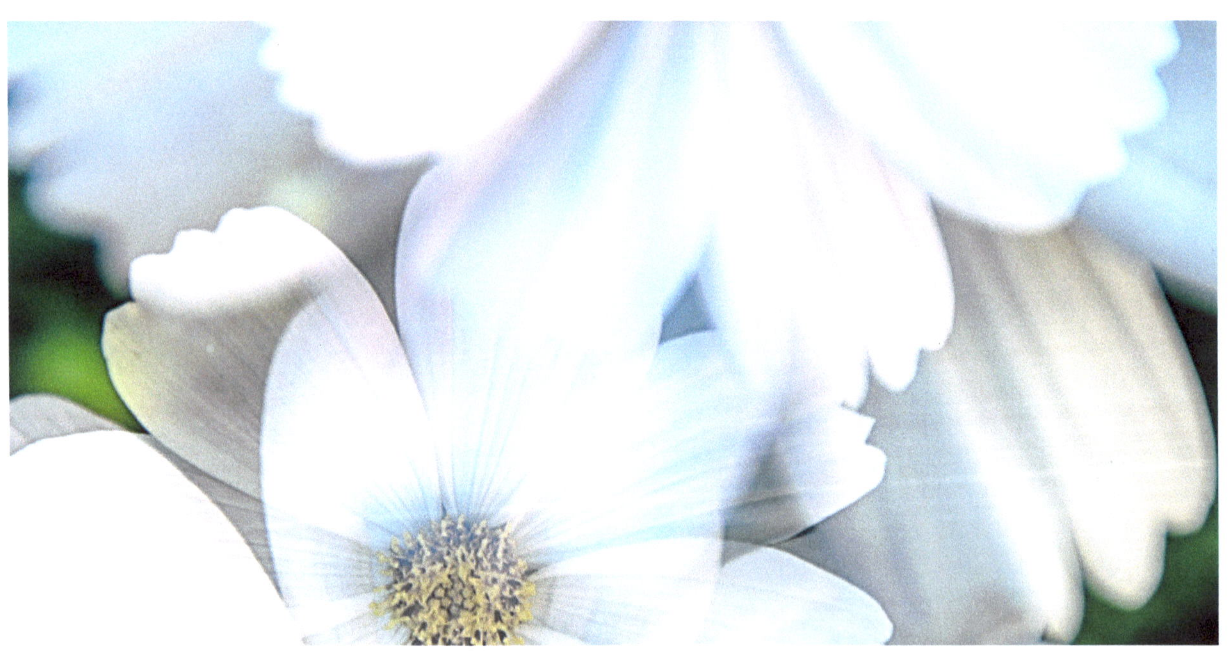

*the love of my life, Anne, in this and the next . . .*

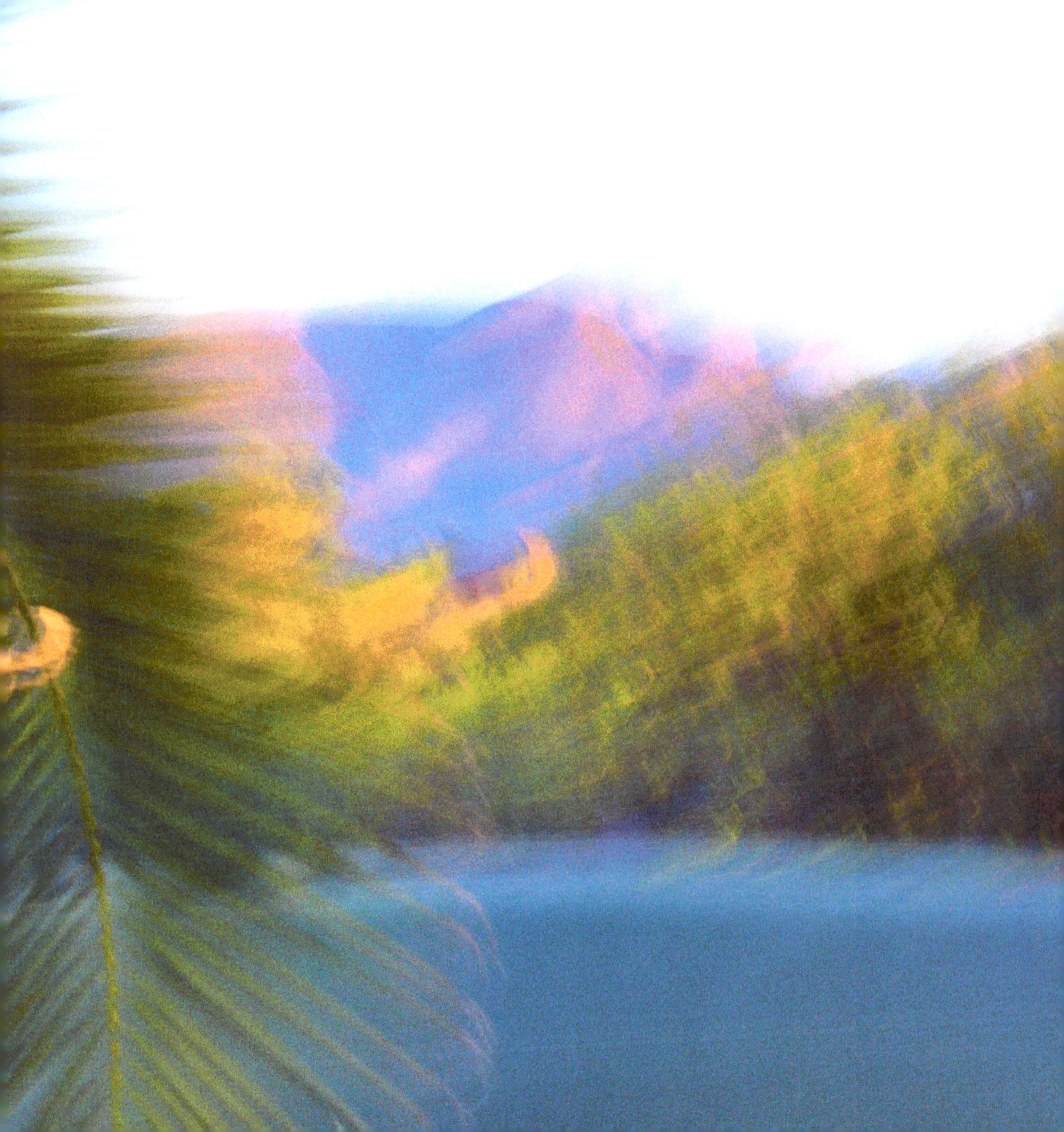

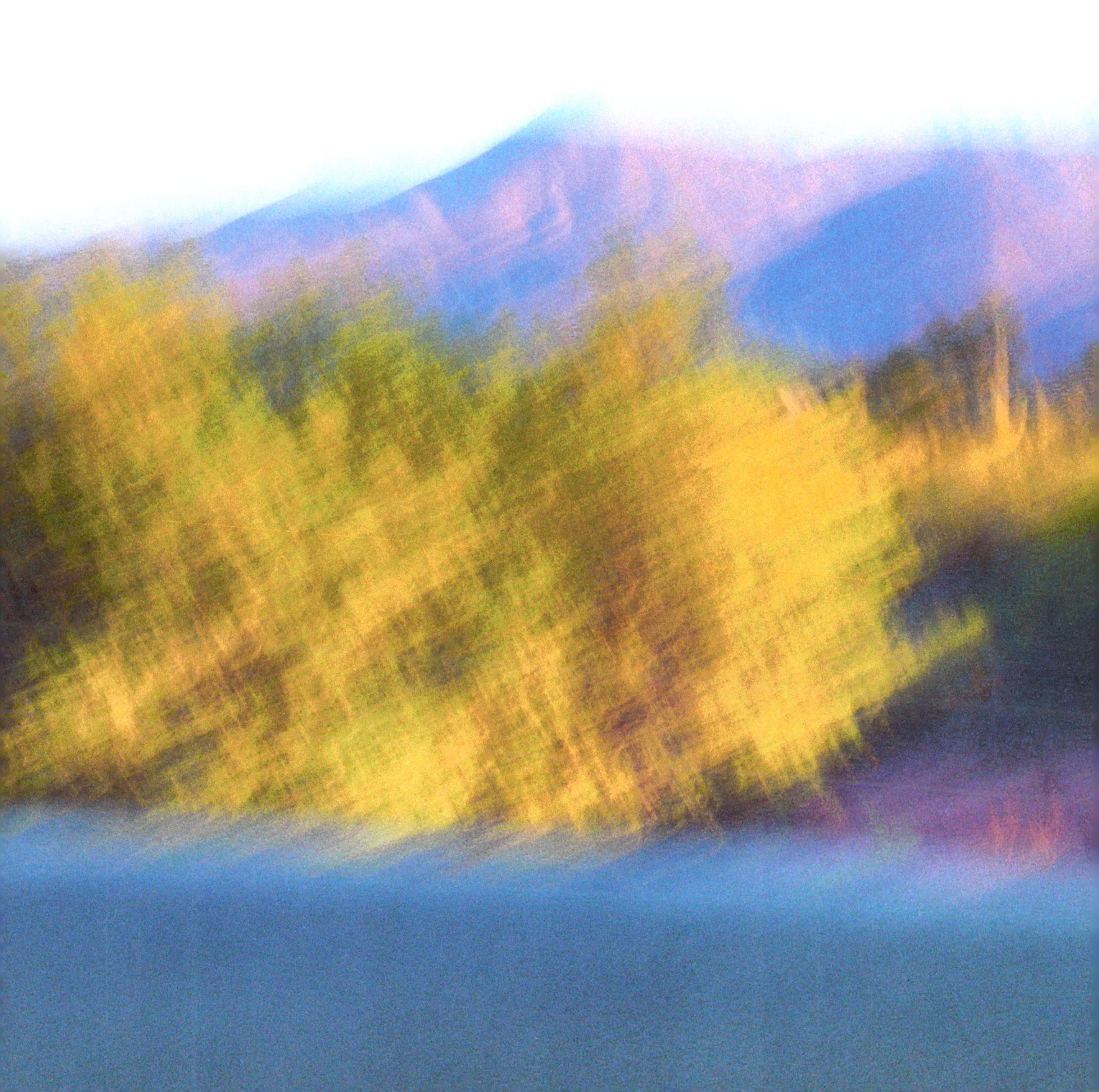

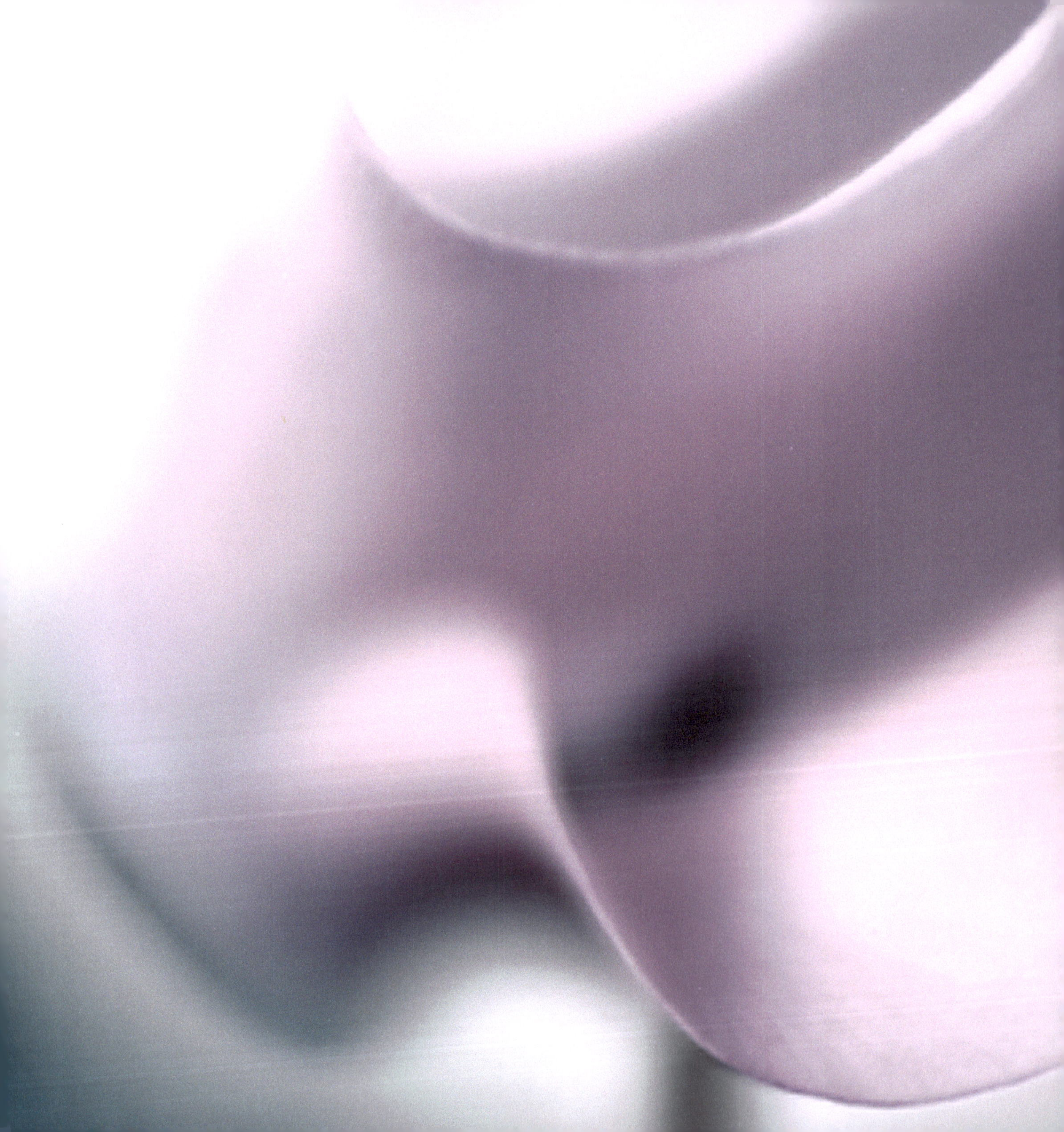

I pray for a life of going nowhere

A life drawn from the inside out
A life discovering its way
A life no longer bound by expectation
A life free of living for the future
A life where I remain in this moment
A life of Presence

A life without anticipation
A life born of not knowing
A life devoted to joy
A life surrounded by Presence

A life so stirring I no longer rely on substances
A life far from addiction where high means staying with the tension
A life choosing not to give in to the temptation of compulsion
A life so wide my narrow thought bands release
A life flowing with artistic whimsy

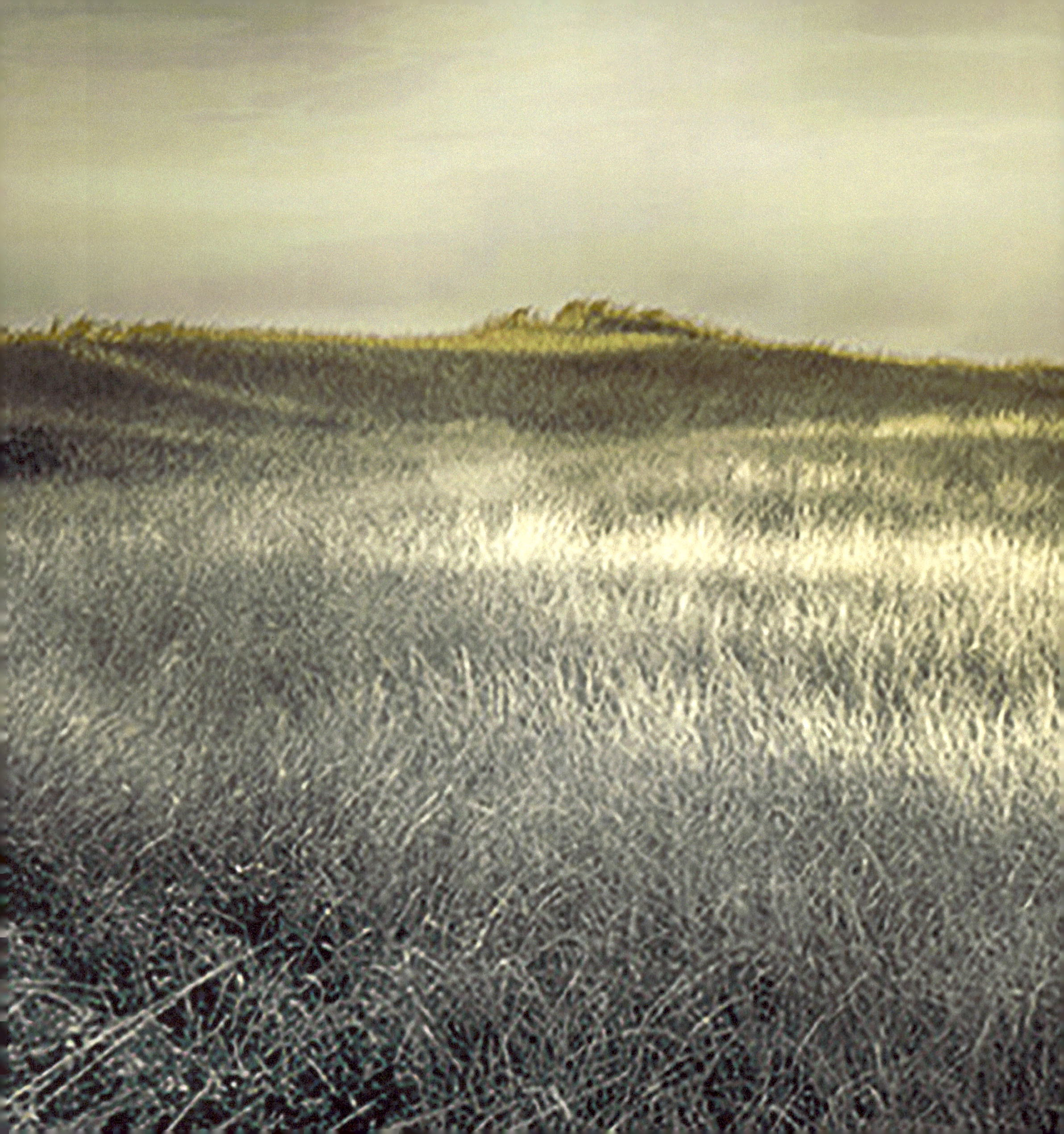

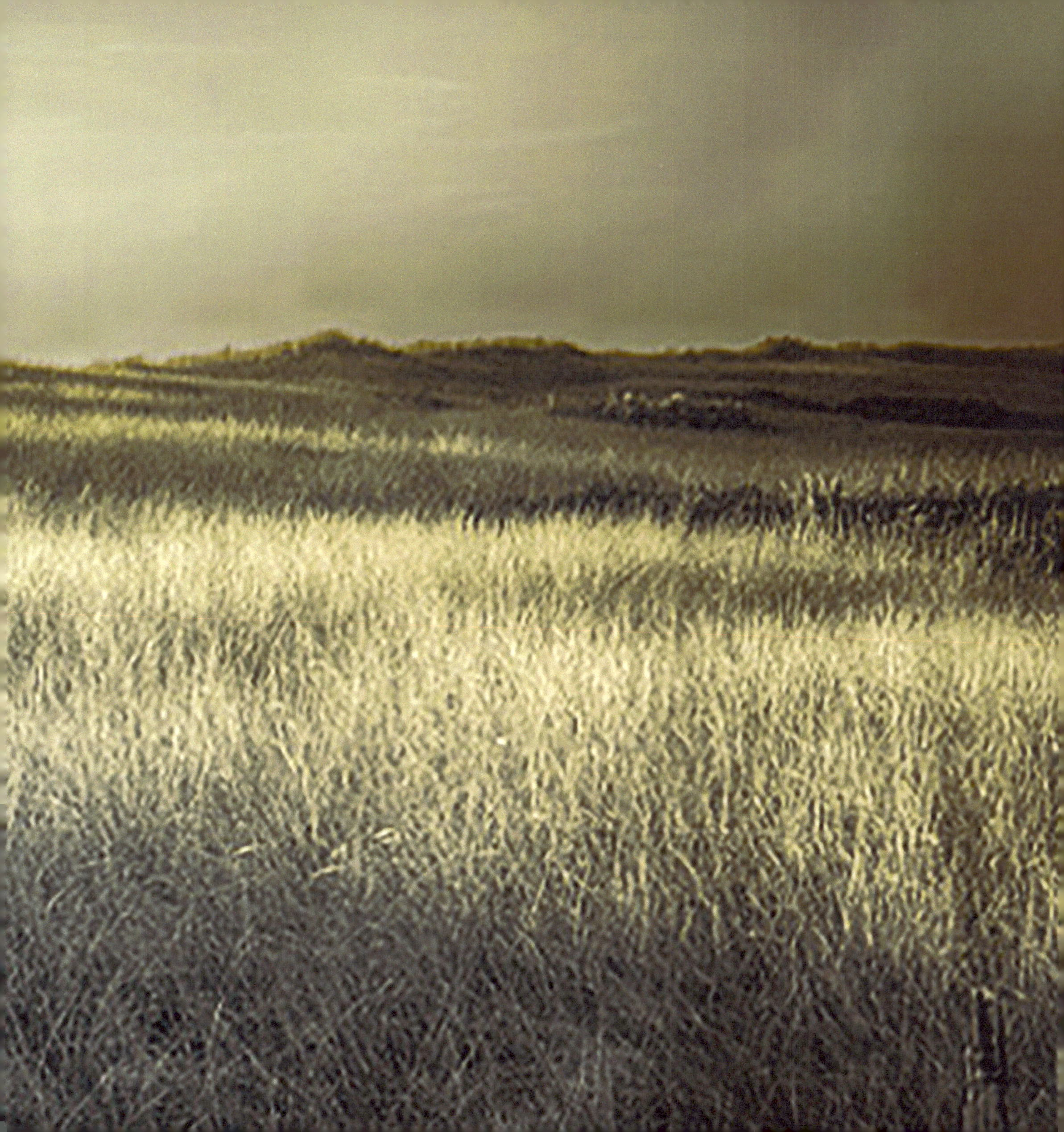

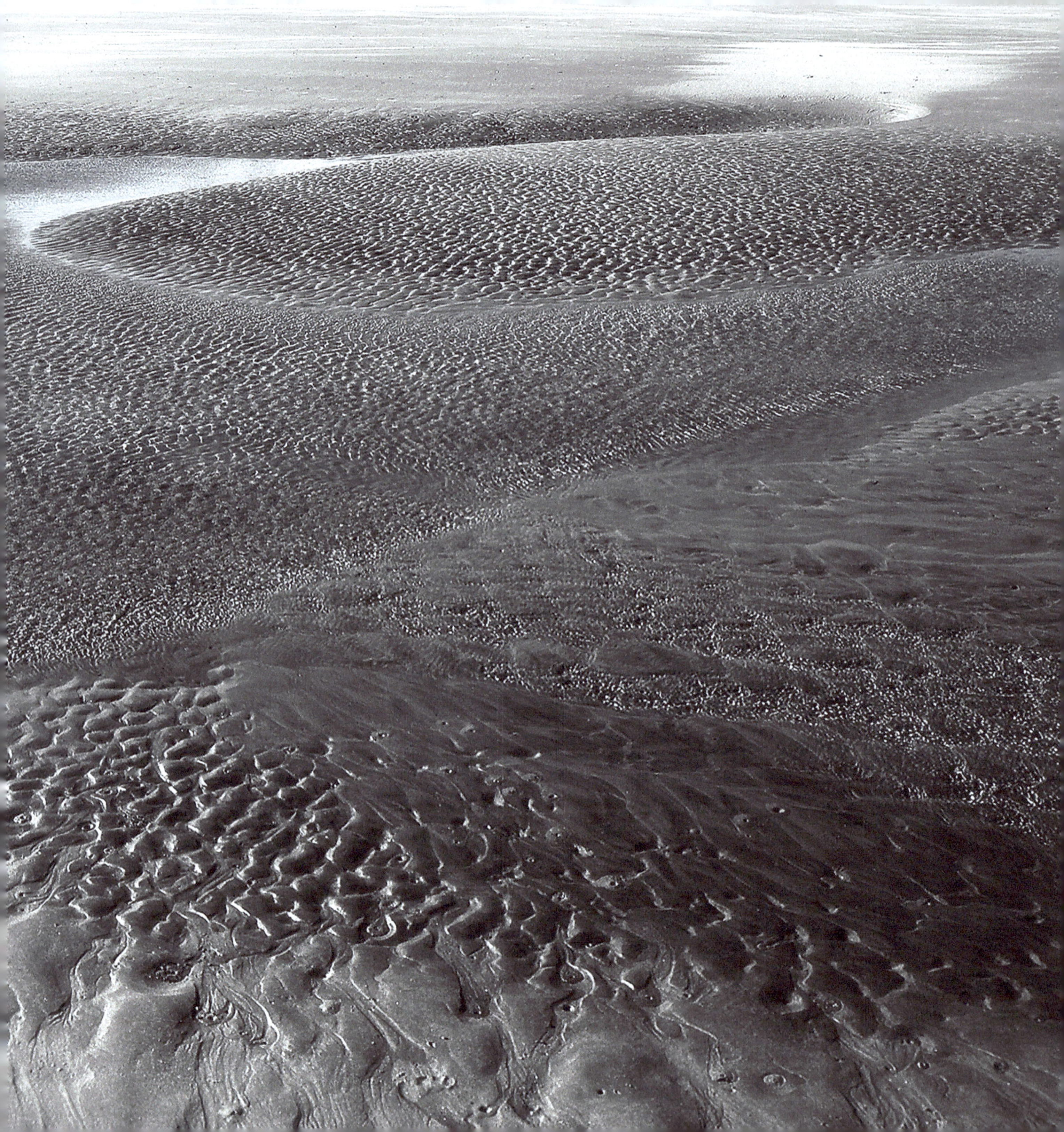

A life free of inauthentic shame
A life without the need to prove myself
A life no longer living through the eyes of another
A life where I know myself as others see me

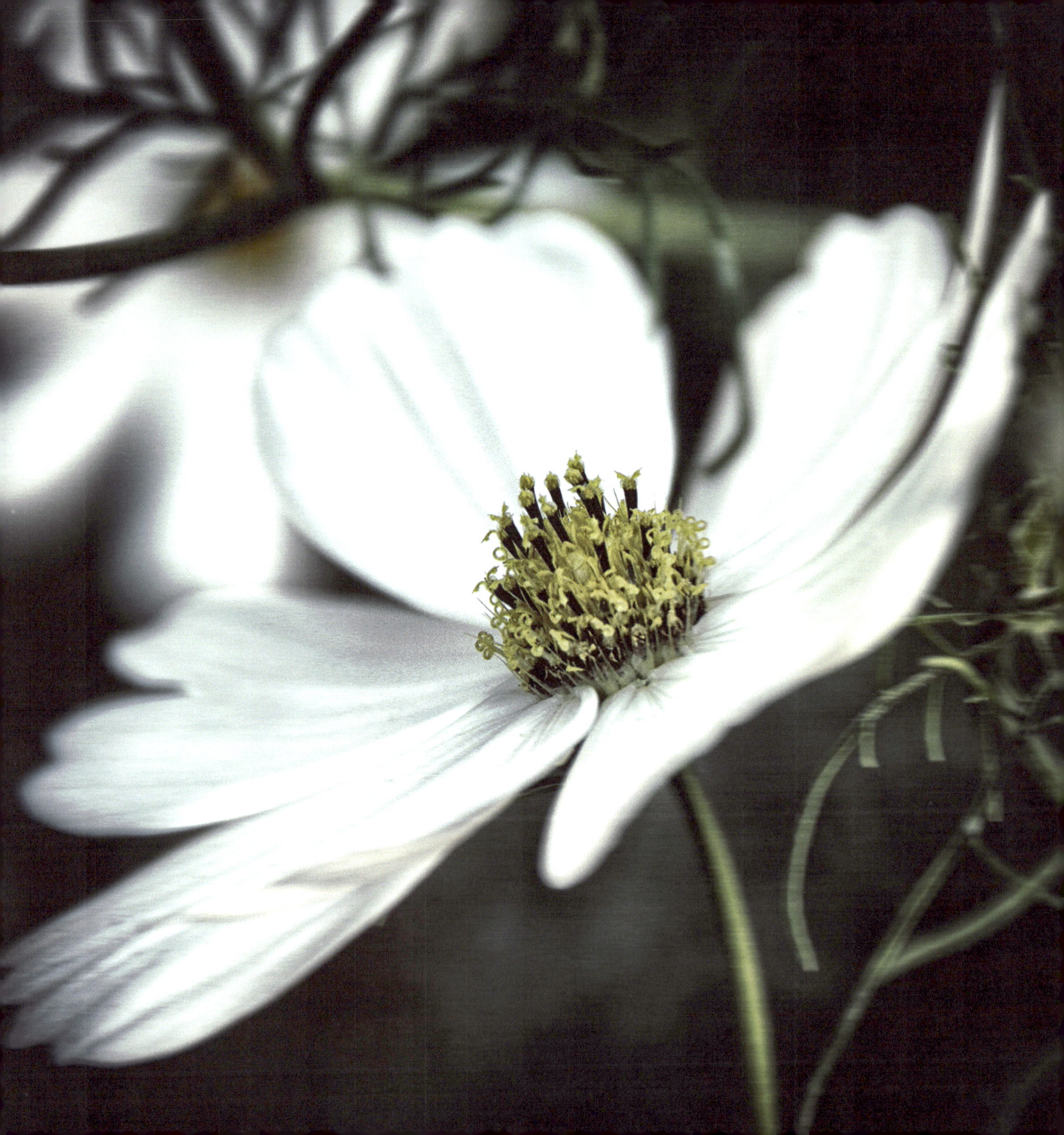

A life so broad it incorporates what comes my way
A life of intensity; each moment full
A life opening to a freedom I've never known
A life embracing that freedom
A life when opinions dissolve as compassion fills my heart
A life where compassion opens to love, the eternal spring
A life where I become that love

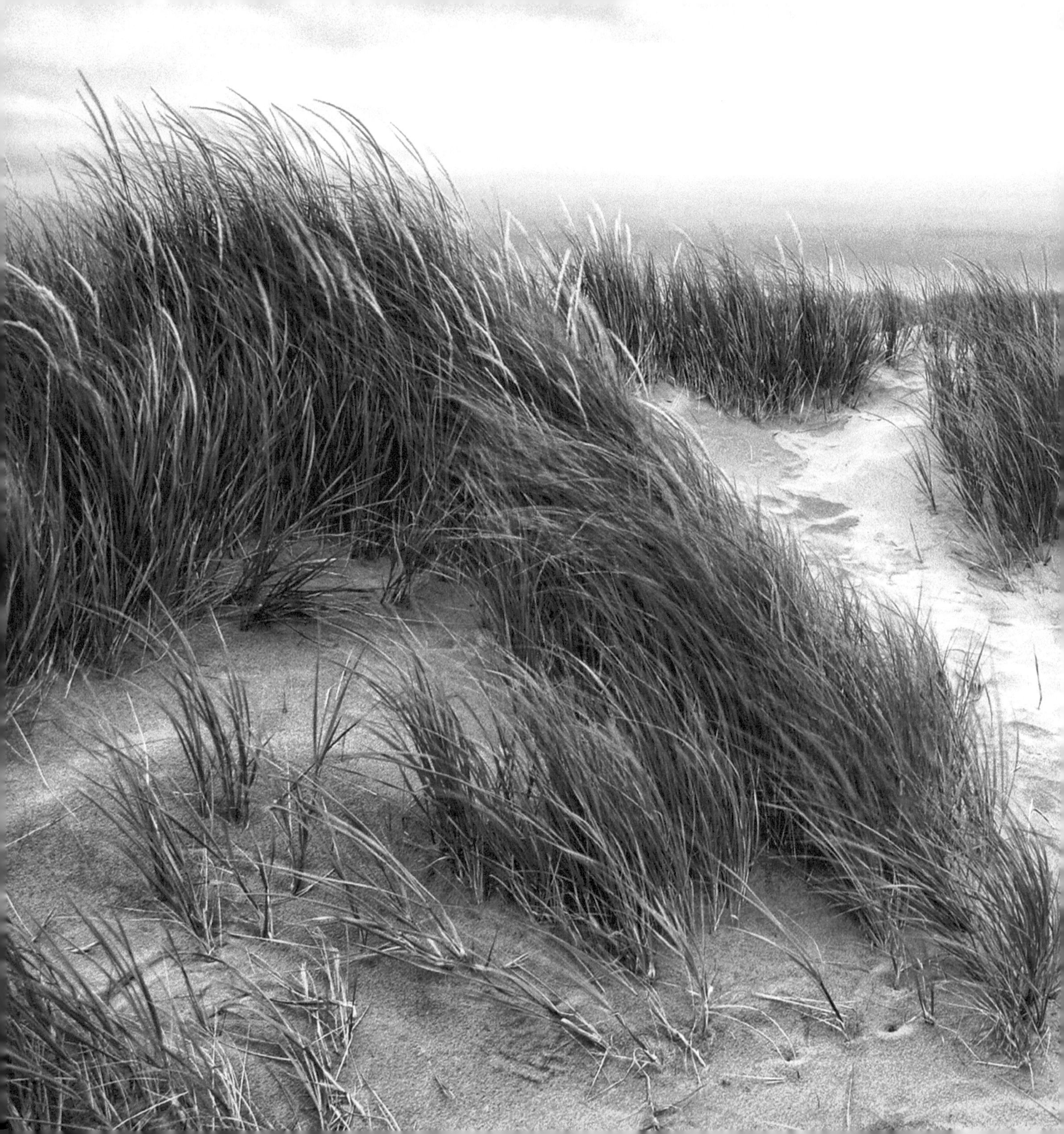

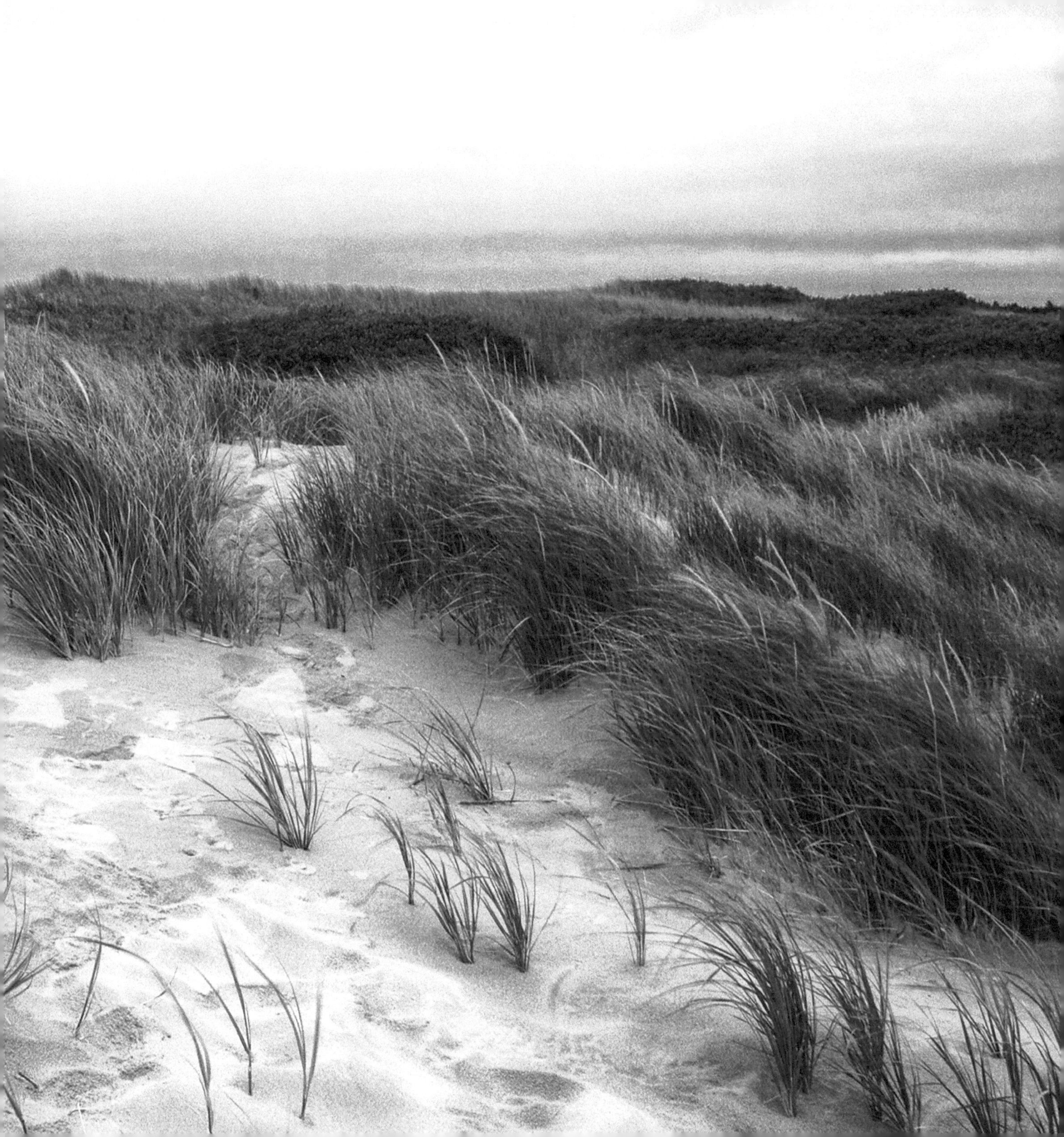

Help me to complete what I begin
Help me to be aware of what I'd like to keep hidden
Help me to see what is blinding to my eyes
Help me to learn what I would rather not know
Help me to search in spite of my desire to remain content

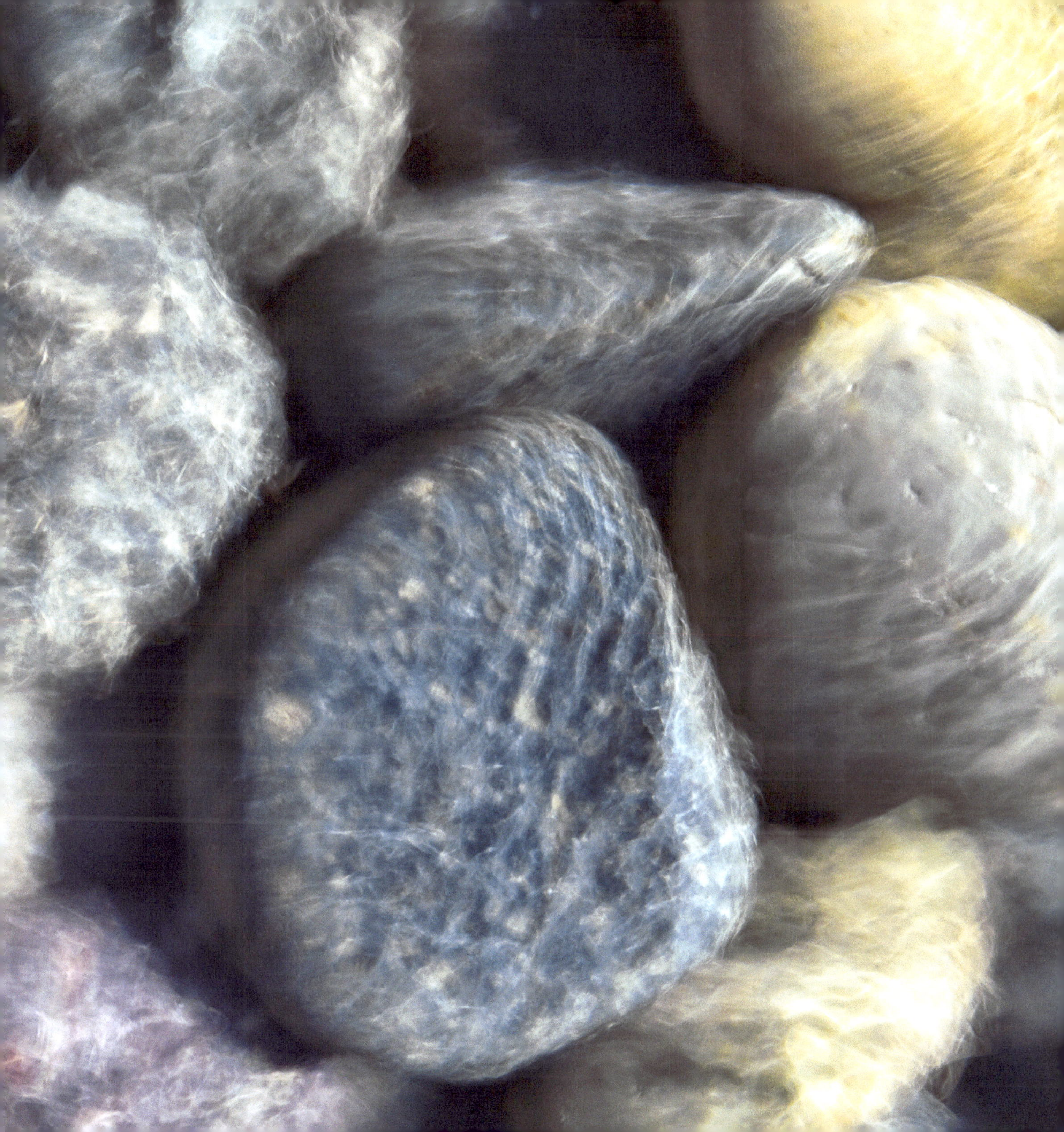

Help me to remain curious after the initial thrill has passed
Help me to leave my old self behind in order to glance at what may be
Help me to travel without knowing where it may lead
Help me to carve a path where I've been afraid to go
Help me to open a door as I wish it would be opened for me
Help me to share a life with You when I'd rather possess it all

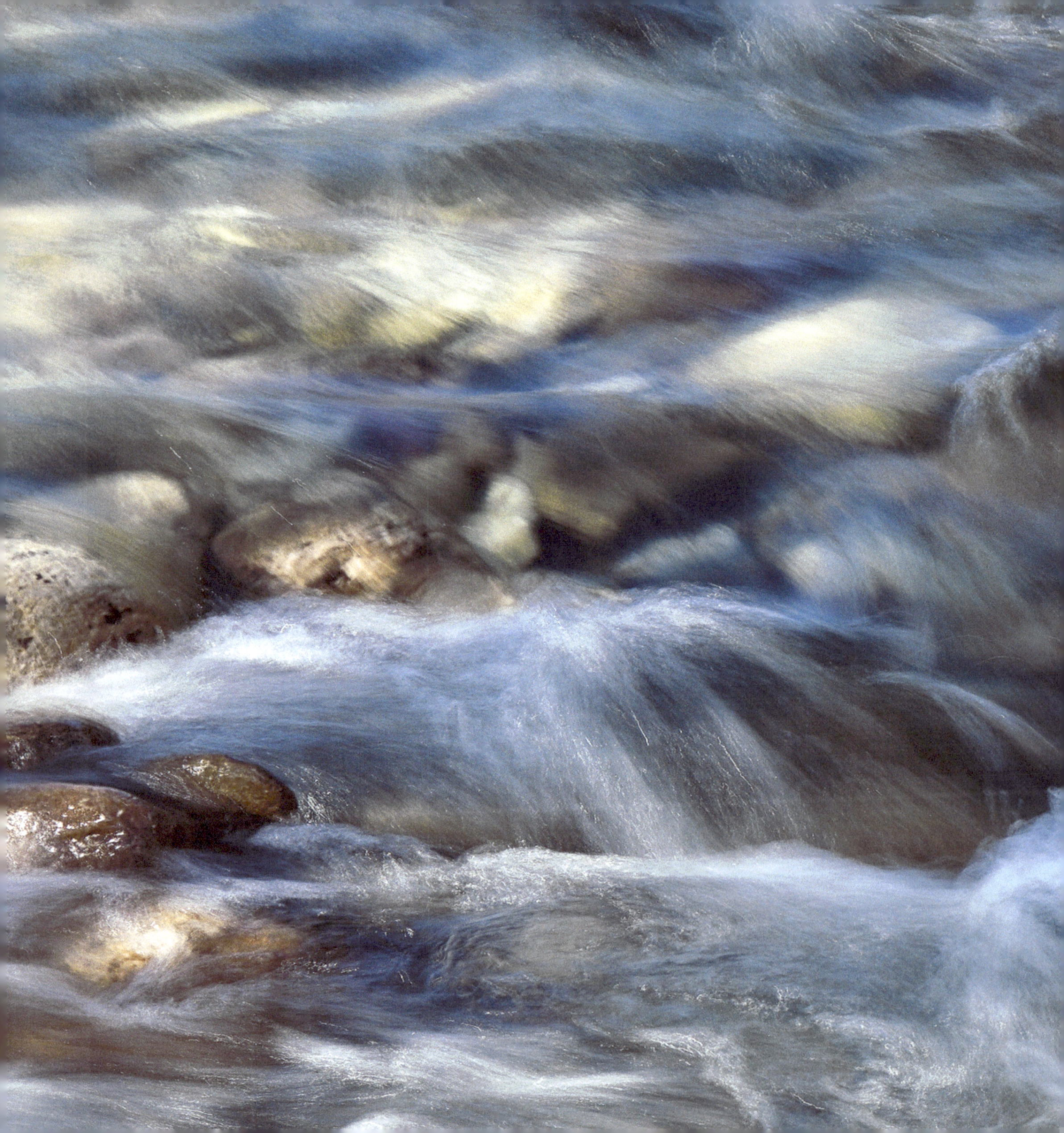

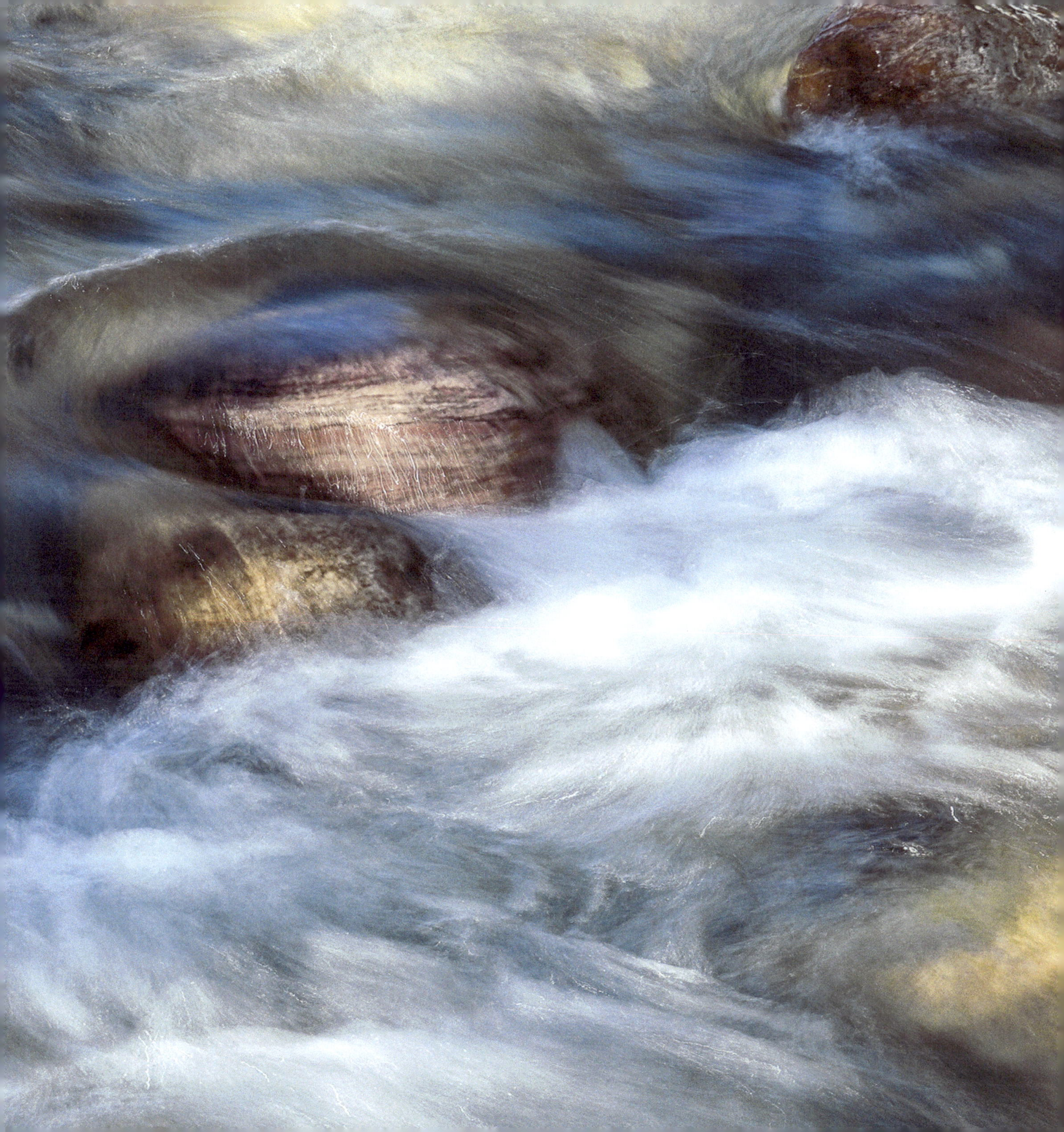

Help me to wake up in order to stay present
Help me to remain inside the darkness of not knowing
Help me to send light into the corners of my cynicism
Help me to break through those barriers I created through isolation
Help me to move out of me, myself, and mine to embrace what is Whole
Help me to celebrate in the joy of others
Help me to fly with Your Spirit so I may discover a hidden way

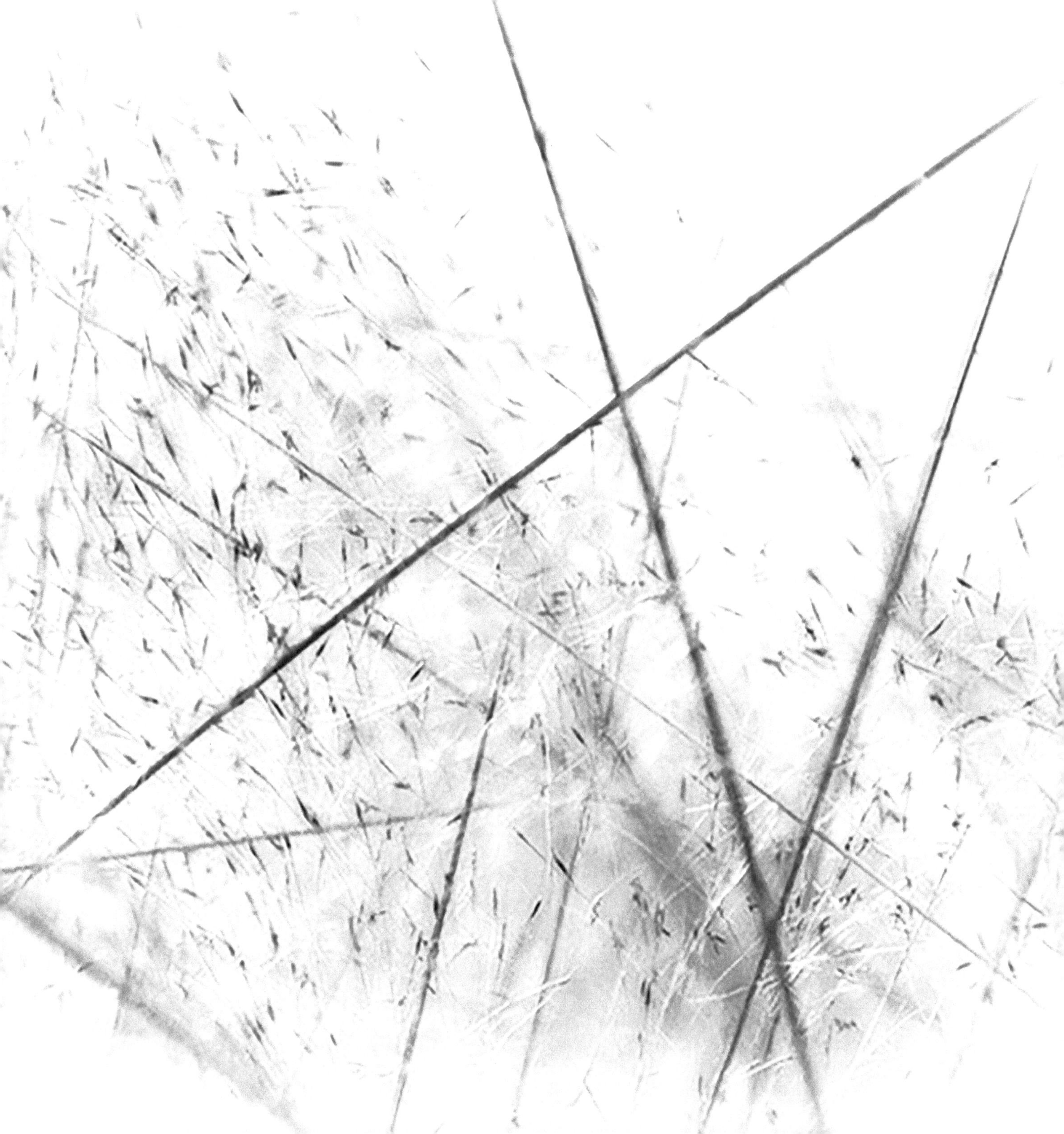

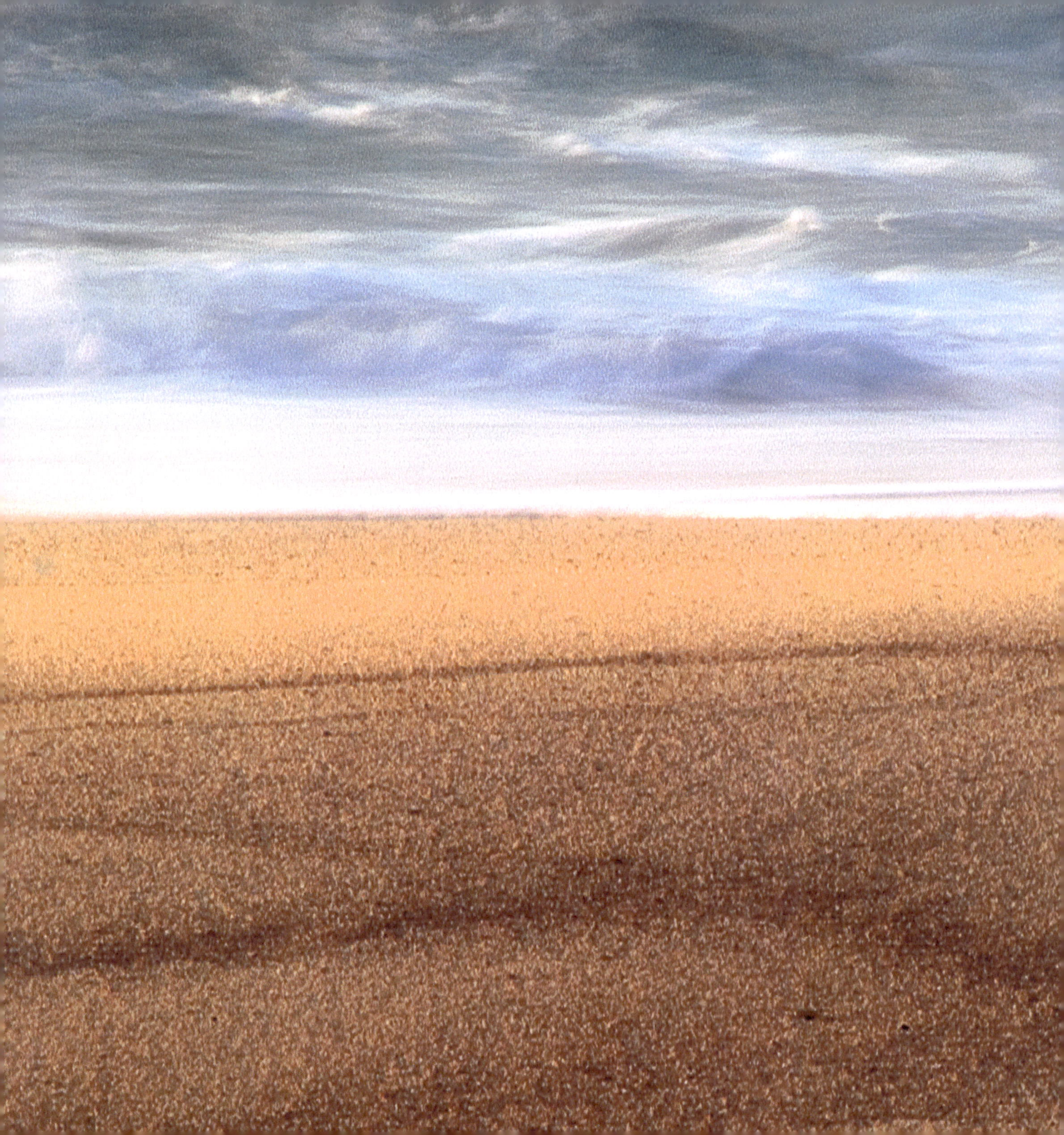

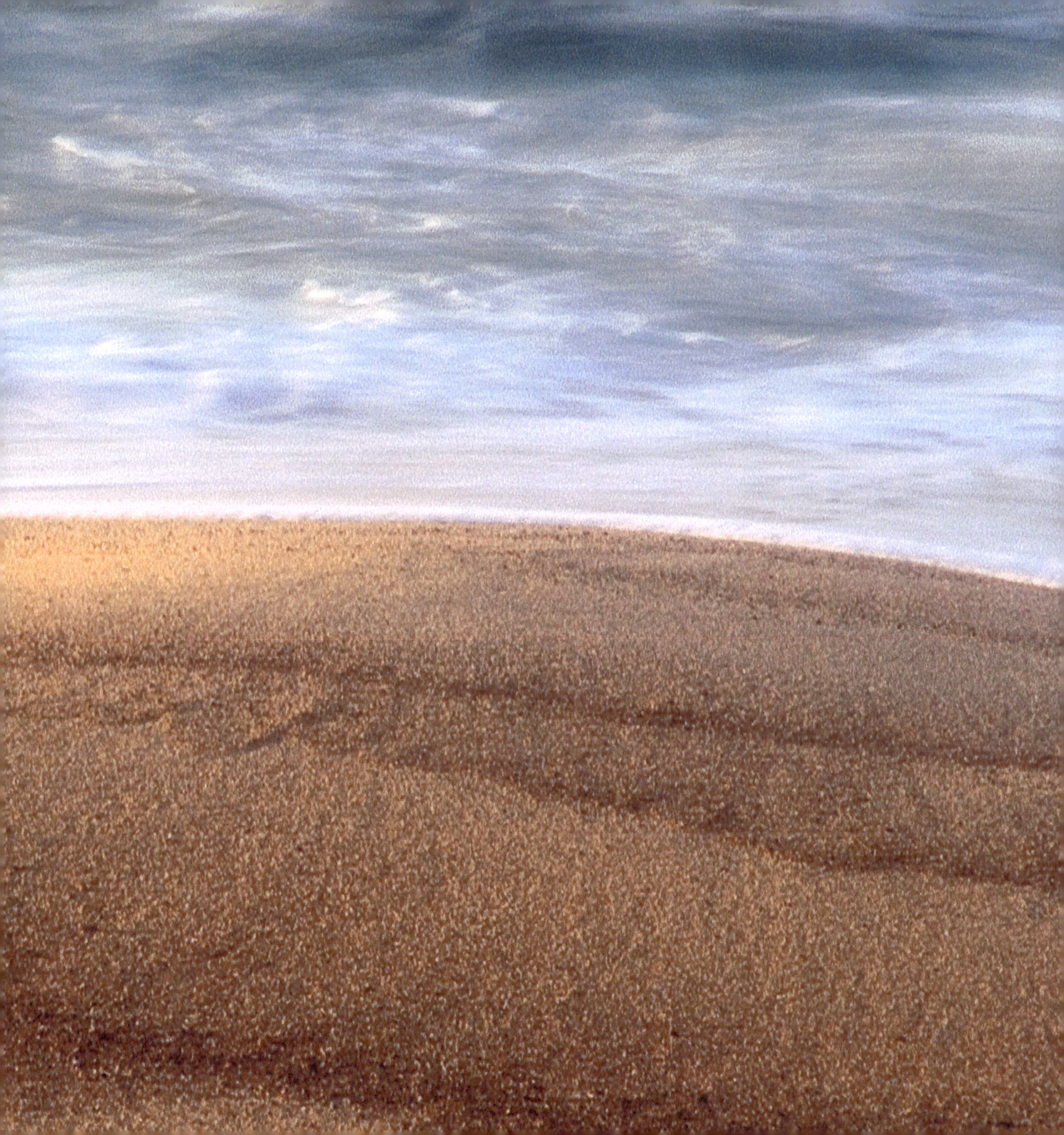

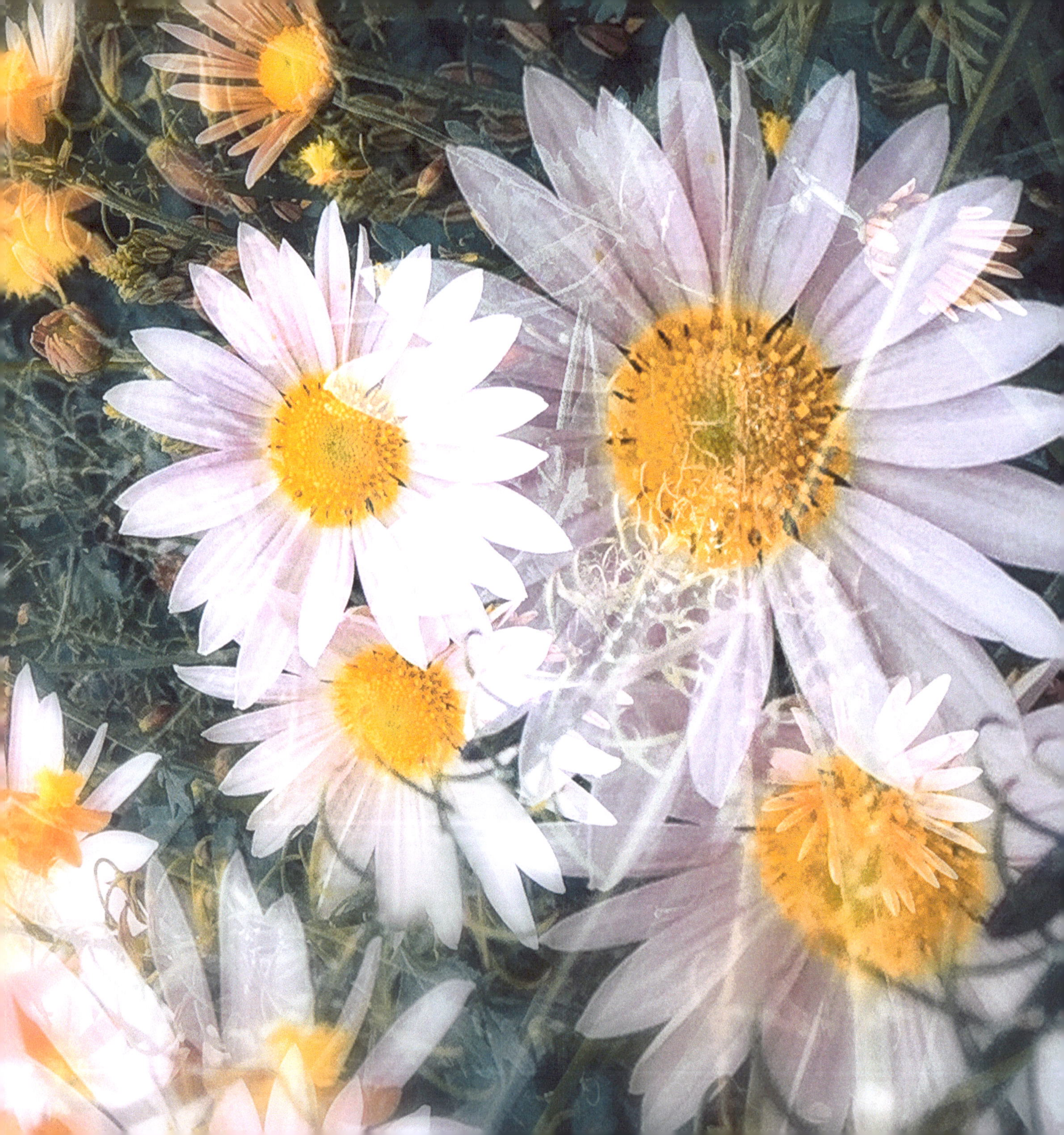

When I stop doing-for-you
And open instead to Your will in me
It is within Your love
I dive into a union so deep
The I who writes these lines
No longer obscures my vision.

This I pray.

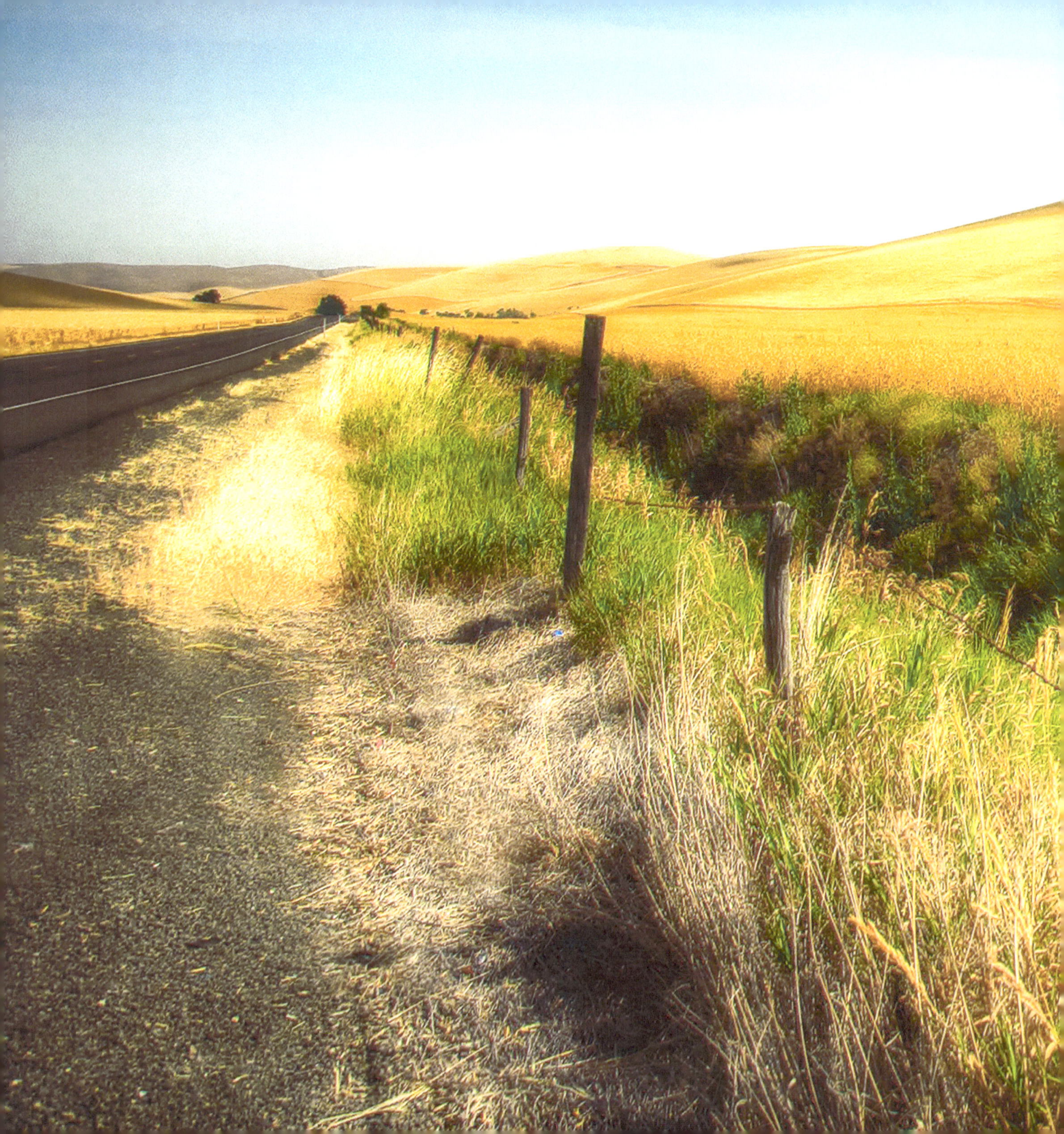

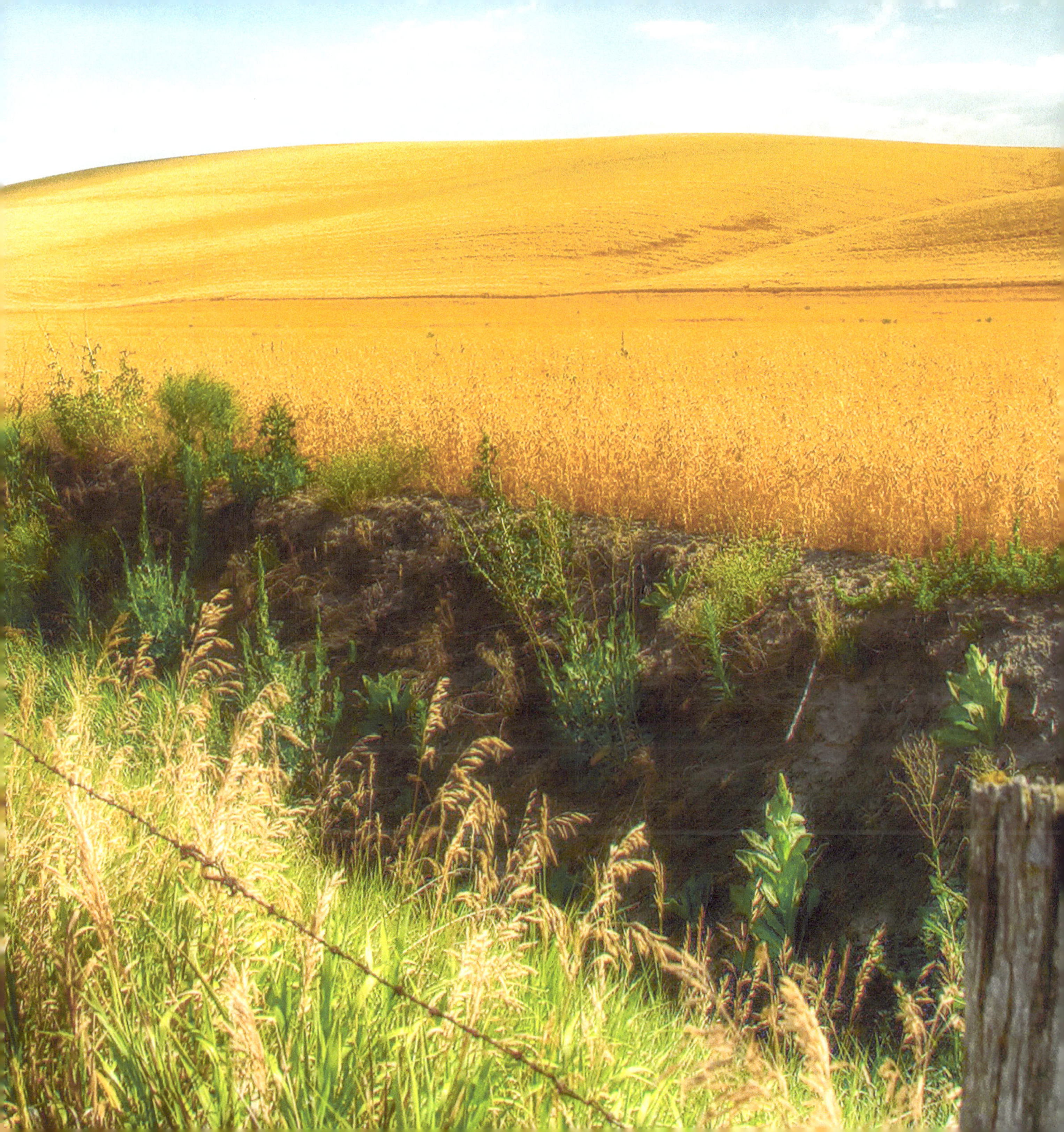

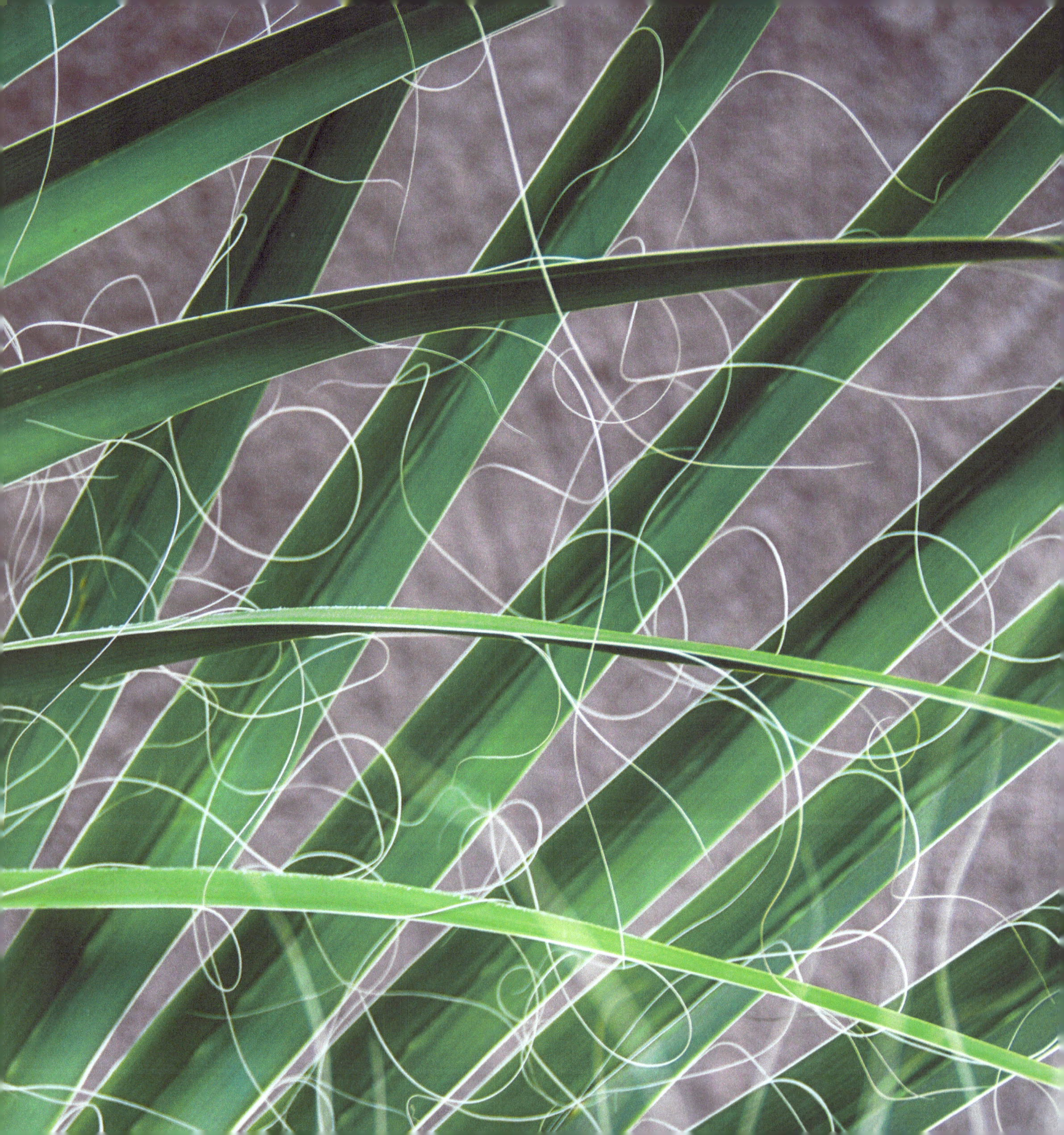

I pray for a life of going nowhere



Published by Shanti Arts Publishing
Shanti Arts LLC
Brunswick, Maine
www.shantiarts.com

Printed in the United States of America

ISBN: 978-1-941830-98-7

Peter Azrak is a psychotherapist in private practice in New York City. His interest is in bridging the gap between mental health and spirituality. Holding Master's degrees in Religious Studies and Social Work, he leads workshops on the power of "waking up" to the Presence we call the Divine.

— www.photographsbypeterazrak.com

Image Titles

Cape Cod (front cover)
The Angels
Sun Rising
Open
Square Moon
Happiness
Cape Bluff
Alone
Open Again
The Long Way Home

River Abstract
Laguna Sunset
River Flow
Sweetgrass
Desert Shore
Fall Reflections
Farm Road
Inter-Twine
Spiral Path (back cover)

www.ingramcontent.com/pod-product-compliance
Lightning Source LLC
LaVergne TN
LVHW070223110826
845147LV00003B/631

*9781941830987*